DIRECTOR'S
Message

As our Nation, deployed Armed Forces, Allies and international partners face growing threats from the increasing proliferation of ballistic missiles of all ranges, our need to develop and deliver increasingly cost-effective missile defenses has never been more important. Our goal is to develop and field a Ballistic Missile Defense System (BMDS) that defeats large raid sizes of ballistic missiles that threaten us today and in the future. Paced by our technology development and testing, we are delivering missile defense capabilities in four phases:

- Deploying initial missile defense by the end of this year
- Enhancing medium-range missile defense by 2015 or sooner
- Enhancing intermediate-range missile defense by 2018 or sooner, and
- Deploying early intercept capability against medium, intermediate and intercontinental range ballistic missiles by 2020 or sooner

I hope this pamphlet will provide you a clearer understanding of where the missile defense program is heading over the next several years. As with all great achievements, it is a demanding mission with many challenges, but the success of our program will protect our loved ones, our Nation, and our international partners today as well as future generations.

Patrick J. O'Reilly

PATRICK J. O'REILLY
Lieutenant General, USA
Director, Missile Defense Agency

Table of Contents

The growing ballistic missile threat reduces military options for Combatant Commanders and jeopardizes the survivability of U.S. and allied regional military capabilities.

BALLISTIC MISSILE PROLIFERATION

The ballistic missile threat continues to grow in size and complexity. Current trends indicate that adversary ballistic missile systems, with the integration of advanced liquid- or solid-propellant propulsion technologies, are becoming more mobile, survivable, reliable, accurate and capable of flying longer distances. In 1972, only nine countries possessed ballistic missiles. Today, the number of countries possessing ballistic missiles is over twenty, including hostile regimes with ties to terrorist organizations. Not only are missiles proliferating, but many of the countries acquiring them are making their own improvements to missiles bought on the global arms market and developing their own capabilities to produce them indigenously. Rockets have already been used by terrorist organizations, and missiles and rockets with better guidance systems, longer range, and more destructive power are proliferating.

Taepo Dong-2 Launch – April 2009

Potential adversaries are increasing Short-Range Ballistic Missile (SRBM) and Medium-Range Ballistic Missile (MRBM) inventories and developing Intermediate-Range Ballistic Missile (IRBM) and Intercontinental Ballistic Missile (ICBM) technologies. With the dramatic proliferation of over 1,200 additional short- and medium-range ballistic missiles over the past five years, today there are more than 6,000 ballistic missiles and hundreds of launchers in countries other than the United States, Russia, China and our NATO Allies. These inventories of thousands of short- and medium-range ballistic missiles constitute 99 percent of the threat and far outnumber the missile defense interceptors we have in the field today.

Iranian Salvo Launch

MISSILE DEFENSE AGENCY'S MISSION

MDA's mission: develop and deploy a layered Ballistic Missile Defense System to defend the United States, its deployed forces, allies, and friends against ballistic missile attacks of all ranges in all phases of flight.

VISION FOR U.S. MISSILE DEFENSE

We must earn our Nation's confidence in developing effective homeland and regional missile defense through realistic testing and on-time delivery of capability as promised.

By the end of this decade, the Missile Defense Agency is developing and integrating new sensor, fire control, battle management, and interceptor capabilities to intercept ballistic missiles of all ranges and raid sizes early in flight. The BMDS will provide multiple intercept opportunities of large raid sizes of threat missiles using multiple interceptors in the ascent, midcourse, and terminal phases of flight for robust homeland and regional defense.

MISSILE DEFENSE POLICY AND THE PHASED ADAPTIVE APPROACH

In February 2010, the U.S. Secretary of Defense approved the Ballistic Missile Defense Review (BMDR), which established the following policy priorities to frame missile defense development and acquisition program strategies.

- Enhance the protection of the U.S. homeland from limited ballistic missile attack
- Continue to develop, improve and deploy capabilities to defend U.S. forces, allies and partners against regional missile threats
- Develop capabilities that are flight-tested under operationally realistic conditions before they are deployed
- Build capabilities to hedge against future threat uncertainties and the technical risks inherent in our own development plans
- Deploy capabilities that are economically sustainable over the long term
- Lead expanded international efforts and cooperation in missile defense

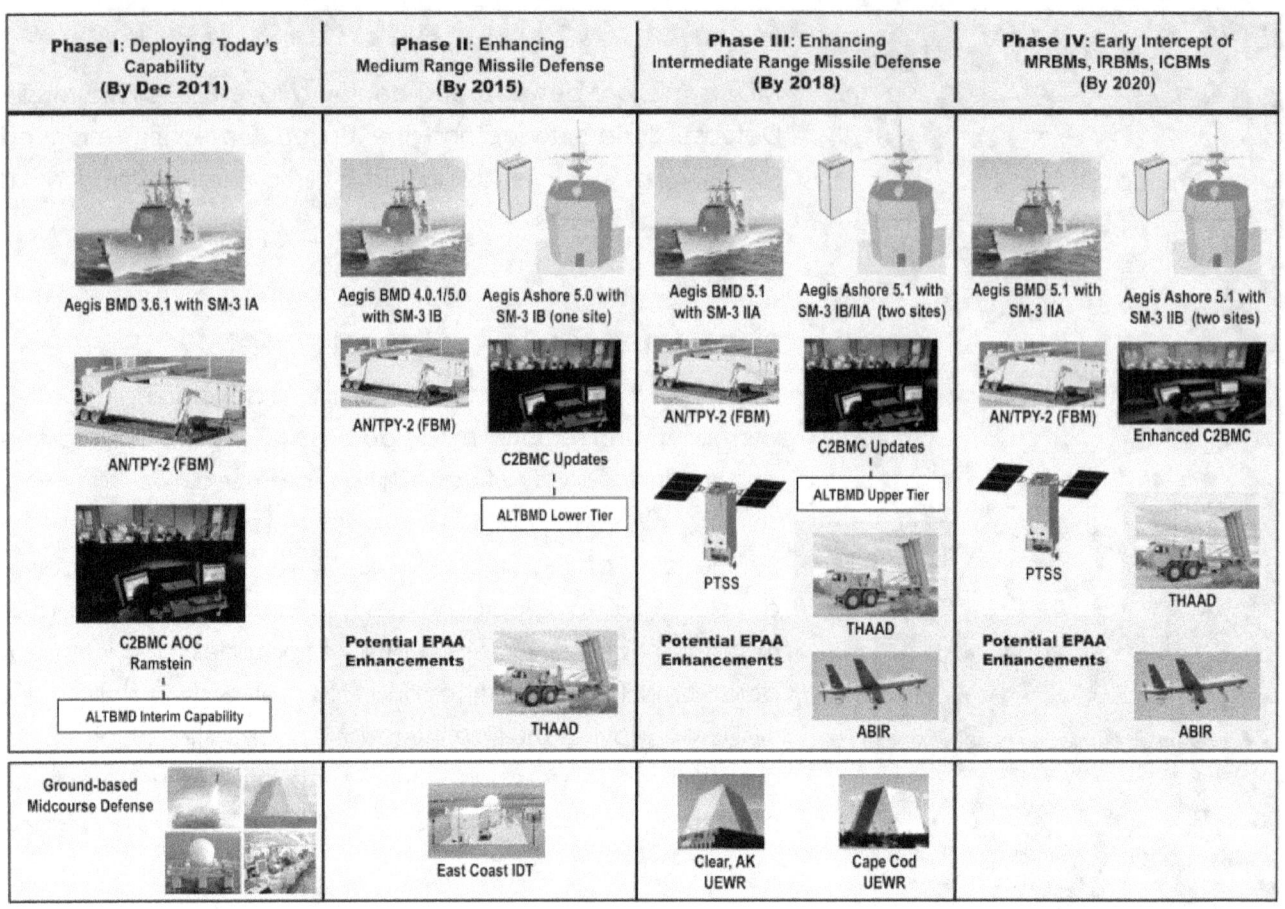

Phase I: Deploying Today's Capability (By Dec 2011)	Phase II: Enhancing Medium Range Missile Defense (By 2015)	Phase III: Enhancing Intermediate Range Missile Defense (By 2018)	Phase IV: Early Intercept of MRBMs, IRBMs, ICBMs (By 2020)
Aegis BMD 3.6.1 with SM-3 IA	Aegis BMD 4.0.1/5.0 with SM-3 IB / Aegis Ashore 5.0 with SM-3 IB (one site)	Aegis BMD 5.1 with SM-3 IIA / Aegis Ashore 5.1 with SM-3 IB/IIA (two sites)	Aegis BMD 5.1 with SM-3 IIA / Aegis Ashore 5.1 with SM-3 IIB (two sites)
AN/TPY-2 (FBM)	AN/TPY-2 (FBM) / C2BMC Updates / ALTBMD Lower Tier	AN/TPY-2 (FBM) / C2BMC Updates / ALTBMD Upper Tier / PTSS / THAAD	AN/TPY-2 (FBM) / Enhanced C2BMC / PTSS / THAAD
C2BMC AOC Ramstein / ALTBMD Interim Capability	Potential EPAA Enhancements / THAAD	Potential EPAA Enhancements / ABIR	Potential EPAA Enhancements / ABIR
Ground-based Midcourse Defense	East Coast IDT	Clear, AK UEWR / Cape Cod UEWR	

Phased Adaptive Approach To Developing And Deploying Missile Defense

The BMDR also established that **homeland** and **regional** missile defense systems will be delivered in **phases** with a focus on delivering **enhanced capabilities** against medium- and intermediate-range ballistic missiles using multiple intercept opportunities by different types of interceptors. Additionally, the BMDR directed all future missile defenses be **adaptable** (mobile or transportable, able to rapidly expand deployed interceptor inventories and readily upgradable) to accommodate uncertainties in ballistic missile threat estimations. As a result of this adaptability, we plan to optimize missile defense interceptor launch and sensor locations by the end of this decade to enable intercepts of medium- and intermediate-range and intercontinental range ballistic missiles early in their flight. Moreover, we will leverage this Phased Adaptive Approach (PAA), to enhance, not only homeland missile defense, but also theater missile defense architectures that will be tailored to meet the security needs of each Combatant Command.

We are creating a network of missile defense capabilities that is adaptable, survivable, affordable, and responsive to future threats.

TODAY'S CAPABILITIES

To counter the potential future ICBM threat, the United States deploys today 30 Ground-Based Interceptors (GBIs) in silos at Fort Greely, Alaska and Vandenberg Air Force Base (AFB), California. The potential development of ICBMs (greater than 5,500 km range) by nations currently posing only regional missile threats makes homeland defense our top priority. Therefore, we continue upgrading our Ground-based Midcourse Defense (GMD) system with improvements to infrastructure, GBIs, and the supporting sensor network. Because of the recent test failures of our latest GBI version, MDA is aggressively pursuing the resolution of the problem and return to flight of GBIs as our top priority.

For regional missile defenses, the Missile Defense Agency has developed and fielded a range of land- and sea-based terminal and midcourse capabilities to counter SRBMs (1,000 km or less). The short-range defense capabilities of the 2011 BMDS consist of the PATRIOT Advanced Capability-3 (PAC-3), Terminal High Altitude Area Defense (THAAD), and Aegis BMD (Standard Missile-2, or SM-2, Block IV interceptor for terminal defense, and the SM-3 IA interceptor for longer SRBM defense).

The THAAD and Aegis BMD capabilities (Aegis Weapon System 3.6.1, SM-3IA, and the SPY-1 radar) are able to counter SRBMs and MRBMs (up to 3,000 km) to protect deployed forces, critical assets on allied territory, and population centers. The intercept of an IRBM in April 2011 by Aegis Weapon System version 3.6.1 and an SM-3 IA interceptor demonstrated the robustness of our currently deployed missile defense systems.

THAAD's ability to intercept missiles inside and outside the Earth's atmosphere makes effective countermeasures difficult for adversaries to deploy, as the distinction between light-weight decoys and heavier reentry vehicles is evident as they enter the earth's atmosphere at about 100 km altitude. Additionally, THAAD's rapid, air-transportable deployment capability is unique. A battery can fully deploy to operational status four hours after reaching an unimproved site. In May 2008, the U.S. Army activated the first THAAD battery at Fort

Bliss, Texas. The Army also activated a second THAAD battery in October 2009, which is scheduled to complete training by the end of calendar year 2011.

The Aegis air and missile defense weapon system consists of sensor, fire control, and missile guidance for the SM-2 air and cruise missile defense interceptors deployed on Aegis BMD ships that provide comprehensive protection. The SM-3 IA currently deployed on Aegis ships has proven to be a highly reliable interceptor. Aegis, using the current 3.6.1 Aegis Weapon System and the SM-3 IA, has more than twice the exo-atmospheric engagement range of THAAD.

The AN/TPY-2 is a high-resolution, X-band radar capable of operating as a fire control radar for a THAAD battery or as a forward-based surveillance radar that can track all classes of ballistic missiles and distinguish small objects at long distances. The radar is air-transportable and can be rapidly and strategically deployed as necessary to meet Combatant Command requirements. The AN/TPY-2 radar is currently deployed in its forward-based mode in Japan and Israel, and new radars will be deployed in the North Arabian Gulf and Southern European regions by the end of 2011.

Over the past decade, we have made significant progress by intercepting SRBMs, MRBMs and IRBMs as part of our test program.

The most mature hit-to-kill weapon system of the BMDS is the PAC-3 system, which is now operational and fielded by the U.S. Army. PAC-3, which provides comprehensive air and missile defense, was deployed to the Middle East as part of Operation Iraqi Freedom in 2003, where, together with the PAC-2s deployed to the region, it intercepted several short-range ballistic missiles. The PAC-2 uses a blast fragmentation warhead to kill the target. PAC-3 complements THAAD and the SM-2 and SM-3 interceptor families to provide integrated and layered air, cruise, and ballistic missile defense. The PAC-3 system provides detection, track, and engagement of short-range ballistic missiles, cruise missiles and aircraft. These engagements are further enhanced by networked remote sensors that supply early warning data to increase the range and probability of success of PAC-3 intercepts. The Missile Defense Agency is responsible for upgrades to the PAC-3 system as well as integration and interoperability efforts.

Regional missile defense requires a close partnership with many organizations in our government. The implementation of regional missile defense architectures is overseen by the Secretary of Defense, the Chairman of the Joint Chiefs of Staff, and the Secretary of State. The Missile Defense Agency develops and acquires these capabilities. The Joint Staff establishes asset quantities and allocates these capabilities. The Combatant Commander develops the architectural and operational plans to employ these capabilities. And throughout this process the Department of State and the Office of the Under Secretary of Defense for Policy oversee the negotiation and approval of the required diplomatic agreements to deploy our assets in regions around the globe.

At the end of Fiscal Year (FY) 2011, the BMDS system architecture will consist of the following:

- 30 Ground-Based Interceptors emplaced in silos in Alaska and California

- 23 Aegis BMD ships capable of engaging short- to medium-range missiles and performing the Long-Range Surveillance and Track (LRS&T) mission

- 87 Standard Missile-3 sea-based midcourse interceptors

- 72 Standard Missile-2 sea-based terminal interceptors

- 2 THAAD fire units

- 18 THAAD interceptors

- 6 AN/TPY-2 radars (4 forward-base mode and 2 THAAD)

- 903 PATRIOT Advanced Capability (PAC)-3 missiles

- 56 PAC-3 fire units

DEVELOPING THE BMDS OVER THE NEXT DECADE

ROBUST HOMELAND DEFENSE AGAINST LIMITED ATTACK

In 2011, the GMD system is the sole missile defense provider for homeland defense against a limited attack of ICBMs. We will soon complete the initial fielding of the GMD system by completing the construction of a new, hardened missile field, communications node and power plant at Fort Greely, Alaska. By the end of this decade, we will have in place a two-layered ICBM defense consisting of the GMD system, BMDS sensor network, and the Aegis system with the SM-3 IIB to provide multiple intercept opportunities of potential ICBMs targeting the United States by current regional threats. In 2011, we began the latest upgrades of the GMD system by planning for a new In-Flight Interceptor Communications System Data Terminal on the East Coast of the United States to communicate with GBIs from Fort Greely or Vandenberg AFB later in flight as they defend the East Coast of the United States. Additionally, we are upgrading the Early Warning Radar at Clear, Alaska to enhance GMD's surveillance and tracking capability of threats launched from North-East Asia.

MDA's GBI fleet refurbishment and upgrade program will sustain the life cycle of GBIs to 2032 and beyond. BMDS software upgrades during this decade will address new and evolving threats, enhance exo-atmospheric kill vehicle discrimination, and improve interceptor avionics, interoperability with Command, Control, Battle management and Communications (C2BMC), BMDS sensors and sensor tasking.

The United States has a highly ready fleet of GBIs.

As a hedge against future threat uncertainty, MDA will have available the two-stage GBI, which allows for a longer intercept window of time if ICBMs were launched at the United States from either Northeast Asia or the Middle East.

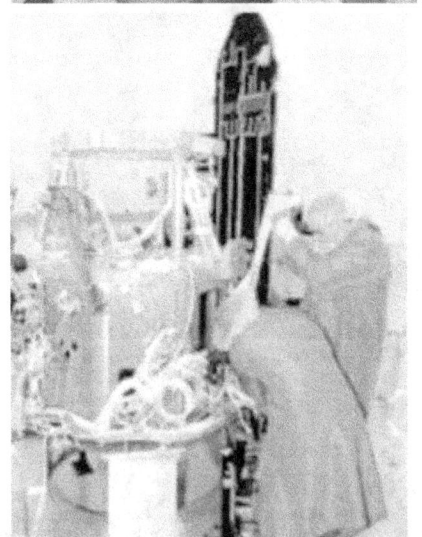

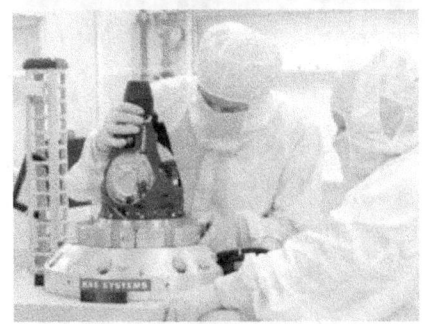

To enable intercepts of attacking missiles in the midcourse portion of their trajectory, the BMDS leverages Upgraded Early Warning Radars (UEWRs) in Alaska, California, Greenland, and the United Kingdom. The BMDS also will receive threat detection and tracking cues from forward-based X-band radars, such as the one currently deployed at Shariki, Japan and those planned for deployment in the U.S. European Command (USEUCOM) and U.S. Central Command (USCENTCOM) areas of responsibility.

Over the next decade, we are deploying missile defense architectures that integrate endo-atmospheric and exo-atmospheric missile interceptor systems with ground, space, sea, and airborne sensors connected and managed by a rapid, high-capacity C2BMC network.

Comprising ground and sea-based radars, sensors on Remotely Piloted Vehicles, and tracking of reentry vehicles from space with Precision Tracking Space System (PTSS) satellites, our robust network of sensors will expand the engagement zones of Ground-Based Interceptors and enable the effectiveness of longer range, higher velocity Aegis SM-3 interceptors to destroy threat missiles in the pre-apogee portion of their trajectory. In addition to enhancing homeland defense, PTSS sensors will complement airborne and terrestrial-based sensors, making it easier to surge missile defense capabilities into different regions of the world.

Advanced discrimination software and technologies will improve system performance in all phases of engagement. With enhanced C2BMC, we will have a net-centric, Service-oriented architecture that can rapidly fuse data from multiple sensors and provide data to distributed fire control systems. Over the next decade, the BMDS increasingly will be able to execute an early intercept, shoot-look-shoot tactic, force less effective deployment of countermeasures, minimize the potential impact of debris, and reduce the number of interceptors required to defeat a raid of threat missiles.

ROBUST REGIONAL DEFENSE

Defending against regional missile threats involves short flight times and requires a highly agile missile defense system with high capacity command and fire control systems. Given the proliferation of short-, medium-, and intermediate-range ballistic missiles, effective regional missile defenses require sufficient quantities of interceptors to confidently defeat those threats. In regions where ballistic missile threats are a concern, the Combatant Commanders are establishing command and control infrastructures to facilitate the surge of mobile and transportable missile defense assets when needed.

As stated earlier, we are developing missile defense capabilities in phases focused on enhancing our capability against MRBMs, IRBMs, and ICBMs over the next decade according to a **Phased Adaptive Approach** to developing our missile defense capability. When the PAA is applied to deployments in a specific region for protection of regional populations and assets, we add the name of the region, such as the **European** Phased Adaptive Approach (EPAA), announced by the President in September 2009. The first phase of the EPAA counters short-, medium- and intermediate-range ballistic missile threats to **European** allies and features an Aegis 3.6.1 ship, a upgraded command and control suite, and a forward-deployed radar in Southern Europe to provide early and precise tracks of threat missiles from the Middle East. The Northeast Asia PAA (or NPAA) and Southwest Asia PAA (or SPAA) are currently in development.

Development of effective regional defenses requires we further integrate current integrated terminal air and missile defense capabilities provided by the PAC-3 and SM-2 Block IV interceptors, with the BMDS sensor and battle management system to expand the engagement battle space. Key to increasing the areas defended against ballistic missile attack, the Aegis fire control system is being upgraded to launch an SM-3 interceptor based on remote (external to the ship) sensor data. No longer constrained by the range of the Aegis SPY-1 radar to detect an incoming missile, SM-3s (using Aegis BMD 4.0.1 fire control software) will be launched sooner in a threat missile's flight.

The BMDS integrates assets on land, at sea, in the air, and in space into a layered, net-centric homeland and regional defense.

USS Monterey "First EPAA BMD Ship"

The European Phased Adaptive Approach is the application of the Phased Adaptive Approach to developing missile defense to specific requirements of protecting Europe.

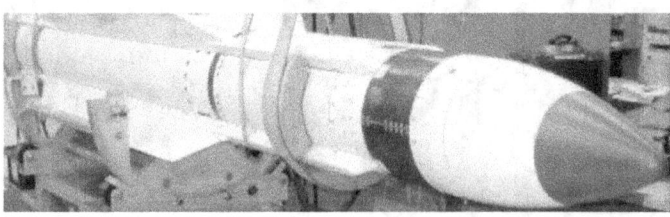

We demonstrated this architecture in April 2011 during an intercept of an IRBM with the Aegis 3.6.1 fire control software. To complement the upgrades to the Aegis Weapon System, we are developing the SM-3 IB interceptor with advanced discrimination and the SM-3 IIA interceptor (developed with our Japanese partners) to achieve increased range of intercepts. EPAA Phase 2 and Phase 3 capabilities will provide improved protection of Europe from ballistic missile threats, to include IRBM threats, with the deployment of the SM-3 IB and SM-3 IIA at sea and at Aegis Ashore sites in Romania (2015) and Poland (2018).

In addition to the Aegis system, we are fielding a rapidly deployable regional defense system, THAAD, that will be fully integrated over the next decade to leverage the sensors and communications capabilities of the BMDS. Like the Aegis system, THAAD's battle space and defended area coverage will be expanded to launchits interceptors on data from all BMDS sensors (Launch on Network).

The link between our network of BMDS sensors and interceptor systems is our C2BMC system. The BMDS C2BMC allows tailoring for each region's needs, and it will be interoperable with systems developed by our Allies and partners. Combined with lower tier missile defense systems provided by the United States and itsNATO allies (integrated by NATO's Active Layer Theater Ballistic Missile Defense command and control system, or ALTBMD), the European BMDS will provide effective coverage of European NATO countries.

C2BMC provides sensor information, defense planning capability, and situational awareness for all levels of decision-making.

CAPABILITY DELIVERIES

Over this decade, we will deliver a range of interceptor, sensor, and C2BMC capabilities in four increments to create the 2020 BMDS. Over time, each capability delivery will enhance homeland and regional defenses and improve BMDS performance against all ranges of ballistic missiles by increasing the number of missile defense shot opportunities, defeating larger raid sizes, and expanding coverage areas.

INITIAL INTEGRATED DEFENSE

We will achieve initial capability against SRBMs, MRBMs, and IRBMs, and enhanced homeland defense by 2011.

Initial Integrated Defense provides:

- Initial homeland defense (30 operational GBIs)
  - New Alaska Missile Field
  - Thule, Greeland radar operational
  - AN/TPY-2 in Southeast Europe

- Initial regional defense against short-, medium-, and intermediate-range ballistic missiles
  - Aegis SM-3 IA
  - THAAD ready for deployment
  - Forward-based sensor data to THAAD and Aegis
  - Limited THAAD, PATRIOT and Aegis coordination

- Both homeland and regional defense
  - Redundant communications

ENHANCED MRBM DEFENSE

We will achieve more robust capability against SRBMs and MRBMs by 2015 or sooner.

Enhanced MRBM Defense provides:

- Enhanced homeland defense
  - Clear, Alaska radar operational
  - East Coast In-Flight Interceptor Communication System Data Terminal (IDT)

- Robust regional defense against short- and medium-range ballistic missiles
  - SM-3 IB on Aegis ships and ashore in Romania
  - Aegis and THAAD use remote sensors to launch earlier
  - Enhanced coordination with Allies

ENHANCED IRBM DEFENSE

We will achieve more robust capability against IRBMs by 2018 or sooner.

Enhanced IRBM Defense provides:

- Robust regional defense against IRBMs

- 2nd Aegis Ashore site in Poland

- SM-3 IIA interceptor

- Command and Control for larger raids
  - Expanded shooter coordination
  - Improved radar discrimination

- Both homeland and regional defense
  - Precision Tracking Space System
  - Airborne Infrared (ABIR) with advanced sensors

EARLY INTERCEPT

We will achieve early intercept capability against MRBMs, IRBMs and ICBMs from today's regional threats by 2020 or sooner. We will utilize the early tracking sensors to enable a higher velocity Aegis interceptor, the SM-3 IIB, to provide an early intercept (or pre-apogee) capability against medium- and intermediate-range ballistic missiles. The SM-3 IIB will also complement our ground-based midcourse homeland defense by adding an additional intercept layer if a first generation ICBM threat to the United States emerges from today's regional threats.

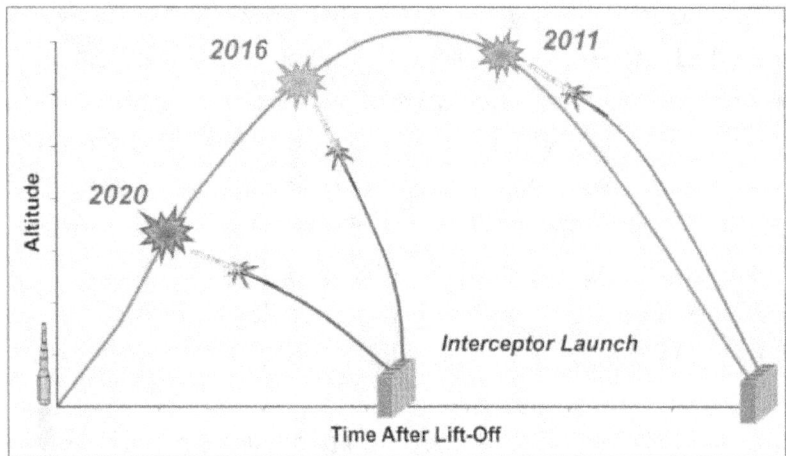

Over time, our test program has become more complex and more aggressive as we replicate operational scenario.

MISSILE DEFENSE INTEGRATION AND TESTING

MDA is executing a rigorous test program that includes expanding flight and ground test programs to test the capability against medium-, intermediate-, and long-range threats to build the confidence of U.S. and allied stakeholders in the BMDS, bolster deterrence against their use, and send a powerful message to potential adversaries looking to acquire ballistic missiles.

MDA is focused on conducting meaningful BMDS testing to rigorously verify, validate, and accredit (VV&A) our models and simulations for use by Combatant Commanders. In 2008, MDA conducted a comprehensive review of the test program and developed a three-phase test development process that focuses on collecting the data needed for the VV&A of the BMDS models and simulations. Working with the Services' Operational Test Agencies (OTA), with the support of the Director of Operational Test and Evaluation (DOT&E), and the Joint Force Component Command, Integrated Missile Defense (JFCC-IMD) representing Combatant Commands, MDA structured its test program to improve confidence in the missile defense capabilities under development and ensure the capabilities transferred to the warfighter are operationally effective, suitable, and survivable. The warfighter actively participates in MDA's ground and flight test campaigns to validate capability against identified threats.

The resulting Integrated Master Test Plan (IMTP) is event-oriented and extends until the collection of all identified data is achieved to complete VV&A of our models and simulations. Over the next six years, MDA will acquire the data the OTAs need to accredit BMDS models and simulations and verify its fielded capabilities and prove that the system is effective and reliable. The current IMTP includes all testing requirements for EPAA Phases 1 through 3, which include 75 flight tests and 102 ground tests from FY 2011 through FY 2022.

Additionally, our goal is to conduct two critical ground tests to demonstrate the EPAA Phase 1 capability to defend European allies and deployed forces from multiple and simultaneous SRBM and MRBM threats. In support of EPAA Phase 2 operational assessment, we will conduct FTM-16 (2 events) in FY 2011 to demonstrate the Aegis BMD 4.0.1 fire control system and SM-3 IB interceptor. In 2011, we will demonstrate, in an operational test, the capability to conduct a multiple simultaneous engagement of one MRBM and one SRBM (FTT-12). In the 2012 timeframe, it is our goal to demonstrate the ability of a three-stage GBI to intercept an ICBM-class target and perform target discrimination.

Capability deliveries will be validated in ground testing (digital and hardware-in-the-loop). Before a decision is made to assume the missions of each phase of the EPAA, we will hold a series of system-level operational flight and ground tests to demonstrate the integrated performance of the Aegis, THAAD, and PATRIOT weapon systems for PAA Phase 1 and all of those weapon systems in addition to GMD for PAA Phase 2. Each

Over the next six years, MDA will acquire the test data needed for Operational Test Agencies to accredit BMDS models and simulations, verify fielded capabilities, and prove that the system is effective and reliable.

operational test will be conducted as realistically as possible and involve multiple targets of different ranges (an SRBM and 2 MRBMs for PAA Phase 1, and an SRBM, MRBM, 2 IRBMs, and an ICBM for PAA Phase 2). These tests will be designed and conducted by the BMDS Operational Test Agency with oversight from the Director for Operational Test and Evaluation (not MDA). The BMD system under test will be operated by soldiers, sailors, and airmen and placed under realistic wartime conditions to independently document the capabilities and limitations of the system.

Each PAA capability delivery will be tested before actual deployments. MDA is creating a series of hardware-in-the-loop demonstrations where we use the actual processors, software, and interfaces with the operators, all of which work together in continuous laboratory and field environments. These environments will help demonstrate system performance and command and control to help the war fighter perfect tactics, techniques, and procedures well before the operational capabilities are deployed in the field.

EUROPEAN PHASED ADAPTIVE APPROACH: KEY CONTRIBUTION TO NATO'S DEFENSE

In September 2009, the President announced that the capabilities described above will be developed and deployed in Europe using a Phased Adaptive Approach. In November 2010, the NATO Heads of State agreed to develop capability to

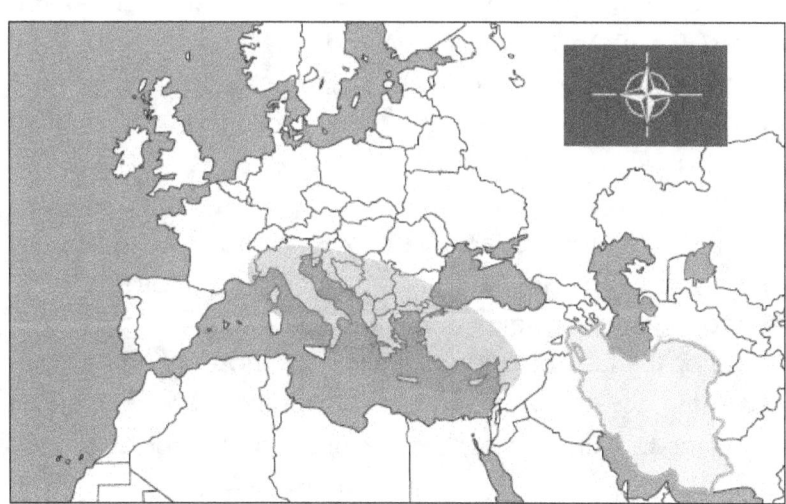

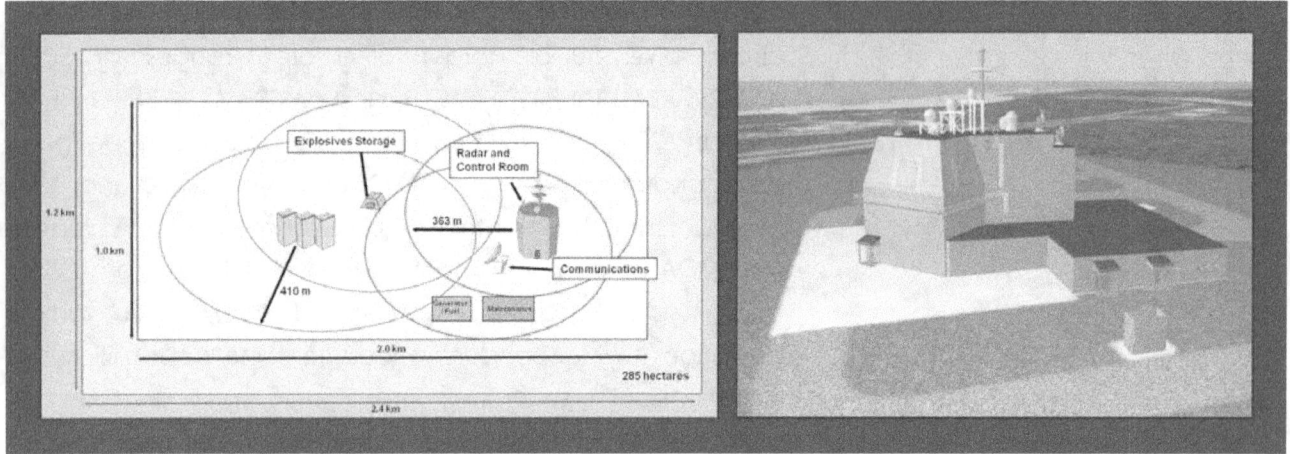

"provide full coverage and protection for all NATO European populations, territory and forces against the increasing threats posed by the proliferation of ballistic missiles."

With four deployment phases, the EPAA outlines the U.S. missile defense contribution, integrated by NATO's Active Layer Theater Ballistic Missile Defense (ALTBMD), to the increasingly capable NATO sensors and SRBM defense systems over the next decade. In August 2010, we achieved our goal of demonstrating NATO ALTBMD interoperability with the U.S. C2BMC in Exercise Joint Project Optic Windmill, proving U.S. missile defense systems communicate seamlessly with NATO missile defense systems being developed in Europe.

INTERNATIONAL MISSILE DEFENSE COOPERATION

The existing and potential threats in each region of the world differ in range, number, geography, and technical sophistication. The nations in each region also differ in how they currently cooperate on missile defense with the United States. Therefore, the integrated and incremental deployment of missile defense capability, as illustrated with the European PAA, will be tailored to the unique political and military circumstances of a geographic region.

As missile defense capabilities expand worldwide, opportunities for international cooperation are dramatically increasing. The goal of missile defense collaboration is to deter the use of ballistic missiles by those countries that currently possess them and dissuade additional countries from acquiring ballistic missiles. Several of our allies already deploy the PAC-2 and PAC-3 systems. In Europe, we are working with

NATO to implement the EPAA. In East Asia, we are improving missile defenses through bilateral relationships. And in the Middle East, we continue to work with long-term partners and pursue strengthened cooperation with other countries that have expressed interest in missile defense. MDA is currently engaged in missile defense projects, studies and analyses with over twenty countries, including Australia, Bahrain, the Czech Republic, Denmark, France, Germany, Israel, Japan, Kuwait, NATO, Poland, Romania, Saudi Arabia, South Korea, the United Arab Emirates, and the United Kingdom.

MDA continues its close partnership with Japan on the SM–3 IIA interceptor (Japan is leading the development efforts on the SM-3 IIA second and third stage rocket motors and the nose cone), studying future architectures, and supporting Japan's SM-3 IA flight test program. We also continue collaboration with Israel on the development and employment of several missile defense capabilities that are interoperable with the U.S. BMDS. We are working with our partners from the United Arab Emirates on the development of a Foreign Military Sales (FMS) case for the THAAD system that represents the first foreign sale of this capability. Our goal is to have a signed FMS case in 2011. MDA is working to transition into an FMS implementing agency status to allow us to fully execute the expected increase in sales of missile defense systems to U.S. allies and partners.

Additionally, we are supporting continued engagement with Russia. We are optimistic our discussions will identify new opportunities for mutually beneficial missile defense collaboration and address Russian questions about U.S. missile defense plans for Europe.

MISSILE DEFENSE AND NATIONAL SECURITY

The United States is developing increasingly proven, comprehensive, and integrated missile defenses. As stated in the 2010 Ballistic Missile Defense Review, proven missile defense contributes to strategic nonproliferation and counter-proliferation objectives by undercutting the value of offensive ballistic missiles and dissuading foreign investment in them. Missile defense also plays a useful role in supporting the basic objectives of deterrence and providing a valuable component of the U.S. strategic posture. If hostilities break out, missile defenses can protect U.S. and allied critical infrastructure, population centers, and military capabilities for responsive operations.

The ability to protect against threats of coercion and actively defend the homeland and U.S. deployed forces, friends and allies against growing threats posed by all ranges of ballistic missiles is essential to our Nation's freedom today and in the future. Over the next decade, the Missile Defense Agency will continue to execute a program that builds on the technological and engineering achievements of the past 28 years and perform a vital role in our national defense strategy.

Fort Belvoir, Virginia

Colorado Springs, Colorado

Dahlgren, Virginia

Kirtland Air Force Base, New Mexico

Fort Greely, Alaska

Huntsville, Alabama